I0412089

You, Me & OCD

You, Me & OCD

My Life With Obsessive-Compulsive Disorder

Derek Ferris

About the Author

Derek resides in the Pacific Northwest and lives with his wife Melissa. His passion for self-expression developed while taking college courses in writing & public speaking. As an OCD sufferer who has slowly broken his silence, he continues to raise awareness through his book.

Acknowledgements

This book would not have been possible without the love of my wife Melissa who was always there to give insight and show support. Additional thanks to my mother Amy who encouraged me to reach out to others through my writing.

Contents

Chapter 1

OCD & ME

Here we go again! Another day of annoying, irksome obligations I don't want to do. I have to do it because not doing it would be even worse. It's my continuous suffer-either-way scenario in the life of Derek. No way out...just make the best of it, don't screw it up, and most importantly get it done and over with so you can squeeze in some YOU time with peace of mind! Balance...got to work on balance. I can't just squeeze in life's pleasures all the time. I have made my life demanding and I'm fighting to keep up. I, of course get lazy, prolonging whatever agonizing task I must do for a better suited day. I'm being held captive by a power that feels greater than me. It's grip so strong that I'm too reluctant, fearful, and nervous to part ways. I just keep on moving forward with my day-to-day living with some type of motivation for a better tomorrow. Give me peace of mind and the rest will follow. The problem is peace of mind comes and goes all day long. Some days are better than others. My good days last temporarily like a drug slowing wearing off. I figure I must stay strong, focused and driven if I am to find salvation. I can have it all, I hope. It will come from knowing what works and what doesn't. I will have to keep an open mind for workable solutions I can incorporate and use. Only time will tell if I'm able to eventually enjoy most of this life I've been given.

These thoughts have come to me as a result of living with OCD (obsessive-compulsive disorder) since I was 12. I am now 34 and have been struggling ever since. I have yet to hit rock bottom...but fight thoughts everyday in a constant struggle to keep my anxiety level down. It can feel as if I'm on a roller coaster ride where at first you're alright then all of a sudden your heart is racing and you want to scream. I've come to learn that not being at ease dramatically changes who I am. I become a more withdrawn person to everyone around me. I am consumed in thought as I analyze what needs to be fixed according to my OCD's rules and regulations. I can become my old self again...but at a price. The price I have always had to pay has been through my viewed behaviors and exhausting private rituals. My time, money, reputation, and occasionally my sanity are also at risk when certain attempts are made to fix an issue I'm having. The compulsions involved can build up and have had the ability to create major self-destruction for me. What I strive to do is limit my need to behave, waste, and spend in the name of OCD until I can't anymore. OCD must always eventually be taken care of and on a bad day it will take over completely. It's a lot like having an annoying part of yourself that follows you around convincing you to do things all day.

There are times when I am even affected subconsciously through my dreams. I awake anxietized fearing the worst has happened. I could have dreamt a situation gone badly or a mistake made that had a lasting effect on me. Needless to say, my mind is always stressing somehow. Constant concerns of what needs to be done and how it's going to be accomplished have a way of creeping into my thoughts whether I'm awake or not. A peaceful night's rest is always welcome when I can get it.

OCD has separated me from how the majority of humanity thinks and operates daily. The general understandings of what is common to do can't be given complete consideration in my life. This realization has earned me my OCD label of approval in the world. Knowing you have what is viewed as an unattractive quality requiring attention is hard on my self-image. I know how to be a normal guy and behave like any other rational adult. I am very aware of what is considered strange, odd, or weird to the average person.

What you have to realize is doing my OCD is a demand I feel I am held at gunpoint to perform in order to have peace and fulfillment. If the OCD is not carried out then I become miserable as a surge of anxiety overwhelms me. The type of anxiety felt by my OCD is an overpowering feeling comparable to the strongest emotions I have ever felt in my life. I would compare it's intensity to being in love, losing a family member, or any traumatic event that takes a long time to get over. My emotional state and focus are determined greatly by events I encounter. It's very draining to have this kind of disorder and I get euphoric highs when my OCD is satisfied. The highs are a result of knowing I can now be content once again. In that moment all seems right with the world. I feel like the OCD has given me positivity as a result of its efforts. Ultimately my disorder symbolizes a pursuit of happiness through dysfunction by any means necessary. The connection between my need to be abnormal and the gratification felt afterwards has clouded my better judgement countless times. It's as if am in a love-hate relationship with my mind. Like an actual long term relationship I stay committed and try to work it out. What I am left with is a struggle to coexist with a disorder which has become the single greatest challenge in my life.

Chapter 2

Crash Course In My OCD

My current OCD is divided into 2 parts: cleanliness and perfectionism. Those 2 parts are what my OCD is trying to achieve whenever it can. It can be very hard for me, at times, to know what is me and what is the OCD. In my mind they both represent tiny threads woven together tightly never to be undone and separated out. I say this because the OCD feels like a part of me a lot of the time. It provides me a feeling of safety, protection, and an overall assumption I am better off. At times I can think it's all worth it when the OCD is manageable. That feeling is always short lived due to the number of demands that can fluctuate over time.

The cleanliness component requires that my body remain free of contaminants for as long as possible. When an event occurs where I will need to be exposed, which results in contamination, I perform what I call an OCD cleanse afterwards. I will not touch any of my contaminated body parts which primarily include my hands to anything considered clean until this particular wash or scrub is completed. I created a numbered chart, which I have to count completely every time I OCD cleanse. The numbered chart ensures me I have thoroughly scrubbed the contamination away.

The logic behind it is to provide consistency and structure. It gives me the ability to clean exactly the same way every time. OCD cleanings are primarily done in private with antibacterial soap using warm running water. If I am unable to OCD cleanse using water and soap, I then will scrub away contamination using an antibacterial wet wipe. This process generally takes around 5 minutes for each reachable section needing to be cleansed in this manner. If a greater area is contaminated then multiple sections are then sanitized, each one at the same time frame using the chart. When my hands become involved it can be very difficult only using parts of them. I try to keep each hand as clean as possible by using my fingertips only. I can feel very unnatural and difficult to use only specifically designated sections of your hands this way.

My hands, most of the time, require a multiple section wash after unwanted contact.

When I am not alone or in public with many people, I want to blend in as much as I can. There are always times where I must behave care freely if I am to act properly or complete a task effectively that involve contamination. This normal act, which generally looks the most appropriate, can result in my entire hand being in contact with whatever I'm avoiding. When this occurs around 30 different sections of my hands require an agonizingly long wash. This is mandatory if I am to entirely clean both hands. This process will take hours to finish if am to recover. During the washing I must not have any interruptions and close to complete silence in order to concentrate successfully. If this does not happen I must start over from where I left off in the counting process. An OCD cleanse is only required when I think I have touched anything considered contaminated according to my OCD.

Contamination occurs when I have or think there has been physical contact with feces which includes human as well as animal waste. Unfortunately for me, this includes unseen traces where there could have been contact as well. This irrational realization has made nearby floors, carpet, and anything placed on the ground contaminated if I know, or can assume contact has taken place there. These areas spread when I witness foot traffic transferring traces from within it to other considered clean spaces. I control spreading by wearing specifically designated shoes that are used on clean surfaces and pairs that are used on contaminated surfaces. Contamination free surfaces dwindle all the time as I witness more.

My method to the madness is to protect what I can so I feel as much normalcy as possible. If an item comes into contact with any of these banned surfaces it becomes worthless to me unless it's able to be exchanged, refunded through return, or OCD washed. I try to keep receipts from new item purchases in case something occurs in the first month. I have found that the use of grabber tools is helpful as well in reducing contact between me and a contaminated object. When I have not seen or cannot reasonably assume something or someone is contaminated then I am able to give that person or place the benefit of the doubt. This makes strangers, unvisited locations, and unknowing people who have managed to stay off my OCD radar clean in my eyes. I am very thankful of this ability otherwise I would go crazy thinking about all the possibilities. The downside is once I'm witness to a person, place, or thing being contaminated I will seldom ever forget it occurred. It feels as if my mind stores it forever to remind me of my limits at all times.

The more I see, the smaller my world gets. My living environment is a mix of clean and contaminated parts. Only I know which is which unless I address it to someone. I rarely put myself in a situation where these do's and don'ts are pointed out. I keep these anxieties to myself and try to prevent incidents by taking matters into my own hands casually so it's not as noticeable. If I'm unable to stop an event from happening then I risk either myself or the other person getting contaminated. When this occurs with another person I prefer they don't touch me or anything of mine. If they do, I will have one of two options to choose from. Depending on what is most feasible I will either OCD wash if I'm able or replace what has now become destroyed in my mind. I prevent these aggravations most of the time by trying to keep my living space private. This insures my door knobs, faucet handles, and light switches stay clean so I feel comfortable touching them on a regular basis.

Now that you know what my OCD is centered around, which is at the root of my fears, you might wonder how I use the bathroom effectively. Instead of wasting time to excessively wash each time nature calls, I came up with an effective barrier method using a folded garbage bag over my hand. The garbage bag is pre-folded four times and wrapped around my hand. This type of quadruple fold gives me enough reassurance that there is adequate space between my hand and whatever it touches. Any excess from the bag is twisted and tucked in allowing for a tight fit. I have nicknamed these hand guards as mittens. I am now able to do my business as long as I have several mittens made ahead of time. The mittens hold antibacterial wet wipes I use instead of toilet paper. These wipes are used and tossed in the toilet; while the mittens themselves have to be disposed of in a trash bin after use. When

9

traveling I always keep newly made mittens and wet wipes in my luggage so I'm ready when I need them.

My clothes I wear are used as barriers most of the time. They primarily protect my arms and legs from contamination I may come into contact with. I only put emphasis on protecting myself with clothes if I know there may be a contamination risk involved. These risks can include anything from hugging a particular person or walking on a dusty road that is of concern to me. This kind of protection requires long sleeved shirts and pants to be worn. If my clothes get contaminated after an event they are removed carefully afterwards. They are then placed into a designated basket to wash. These clothes have to be handled with gloves and placed into a washing machine for laundry. After the clothes are placed carefully into the machine they will have to be washed twice. Washing clothing twice assures me that the adequate amount of spins have taken place during the wash cycles. The spin count is based off of my numbered chart to insure a proper OCD wash.

When it comes to prized possessions of value I must keep them clean to insure their worth. These valuables are either expensive or unique and are hard to replace. They must be securely stored at all times and only be touched when my hands are OCD washed. I have always allocated an area off limits to anybody else for this purpose. It's like an OCD inspired man cave. In order to prevent excessive hoarding, I make sure to limit these types of items to only one room.

The perfectionism component to my OCD requires me to strive for flawlessness by setting excessively high performance standards for things I value. Parts of this component play a role in my washings and storing. They also include how I treat my personal information like social security number, bank accounts, etc. All personal information on paper must be scratched out with a black pen after reading. If I acquire an abundance of papers containing sensitive information will then have to burn them. Any personal information accessed or given online must be done after a full computer scan has been made to check for security threats.

You might wonder how I keep up with these exhausting irrational demands I set. I have to be able to keep up if I am to stay on top of my disorder. Having energy is a must for my OCD to effectively be carried out in the fastest way possible. Attention to detail is strengthened as well when having an increased energy level. I have found that caffeine gives me the power to tackle a lot of what I create for myself. I have discovered a vitamin B/caffeine supplement called a 5 hour energy shot which gives me that boost to be focused, motivated, and effective in conserving the time spent on OCD. Preparation is also a must. When your needs are as specific as mine it is vital to plan out your course of action.

There you have it! That's what encompasses my OCD and how it's dealt with. I'm a man with many particulars required in order to live day-to-day successfully. Without these thoughts and desires I would be your average guy. So what does one do with such an affliction? I already know what you're thinking. I need to first seek therapy and second take medication in the process...right? I have done a little of both as well as discovered the workable solutions I've mentioned that make my life more tolerable. The problem for me is maintaining all of these vital parts in perfect harmony which would ideally provide just enough of each to balance my life successfully. It's a juggling act I've not mastered yet. Emphasis, determination, and follow through have become a work in progress as I seek to better myself.

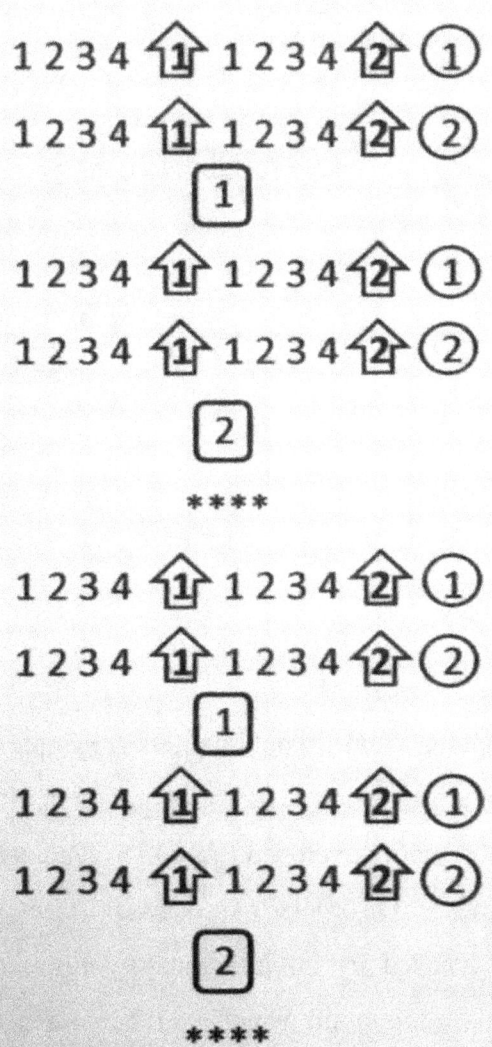

Numbered Chart

Chapter 3

The Early Years

I began having what I would call OCD symptoms at about age 12 after recovering from a severe strep infection. Studies indicate a high likelihood that I developed PANDAS (Pediatric Autoimmune Neuropsychiatric Disorders Associated with Streptococcus). PANDAS is caused by an inflammatory response in the basal ganglia area of the brain which can be in reaction to a strep infection. The reaction triggers antibodies that attack the brain causing the OCD. The basal ganglia section of the brain is associated with a variety of functions including routine behaviors. Popular theories suggest this area of the brain is responsible in helping you decide what possible behaviors to execute at any given time. I had no idea that over 2 decades ago my strep infection could have started it all. I figured it could be a contributing factor I would have to consider. It all began to make sense as I remembered back to when my parents began seeking help for me.

My OCD is much different now than when it all started. In the beginning, my parents started noticing my odd behaviors which included a lot of organizational obsessions. I would have to symmetrically fold and hang my clothes and pants in an attempt to achieve perfection. My other belongings had to be placed in perfect order as well. My bed needed to be made in such a way that it would take hours to completely make perfect after sleeping in it. I would neatly smooth out all the wrinkles as I carefully tucked in the sheets around the mattress. Once it was made I didn't want to sleep in it because it would involve starting the process all over again. At times I would use a sleeping bag instead of my bed in an effort to minimize the amount of times I would have to painstakingly make my bed. Eventually I began washing my hands prior to organizing. The association between being neat and clean would soon be taken to an obsessional level. My parents thought it was just a phase at first and that I would grow out of it. Months turned into years and my OCD evolved along the way. My concerns and obsessions would either deepen or replace my old ones. Perfected organization was no longer my focus. I shifted my efforts towards achieving other desired outcomes. Importance and value to me would soon become synonymous with cleanliness and materialism.

It started when I began to store what I considered to be clean items so they would never get dirty, which affected their worth in my mind. Being younger, I used the word dirty and not contaminated back then. Just like a collector I would purchase some items I considered valuable and keep them unopened. As a teenager these items primarily consisted of video game systems, accessories, and the games themselves. They were expensive to me at the time and I wanted to preserve them. I would need a place to keep these items safe if they were to remain clean and unopened. I eventually convinced my father who is a contractor to build me a storage room in the garage for my prized possessions. He was reluctant at first but decided to go ahead with it. Unfortunately, after it was finished he refused to allow a lock on it but assured me he would not use it. I eventually came to realize one day he had broken his word. I was devastated as I entered the storage room to find his equipment alongside my valuables. From that moment on I never compromised again with my parents when it came to my OCD needs.

After I graduated high school in Central Oregon, my parents came to the realization that I had some type of mental disorder that they had to come to terms with. This was difficult for them; they themselves had no knowledge or comprehension of what I was going through. My mother had always been a stressed person but her level had no comparison to mine. After expressing their concerns to me over and over again, it was understood that I had to get psychiatric help. Prior to speaking with someone, I was driven to a testing clinic to rule out any medical concerns caused by physical implications. I had urine, mucus, and salvia samples taken. My mouth swab indicated I was a strep carrier. I was given a prescription of antibiotics to take over the course of several weeks. No correlation between my OCD and the strep was ever made at that time.

I was reluctant to see a psychiatrist at the time but my parents insisted. I was ignorant to their concerns, thinking a professional would have little influence over me. An appointment was made to see a local psychiatrist by the name of Mr. Blumer, who specialized in child & adolescent psychiatry. I was very annoyed during the first visit because I didn't want to be there discussing my OCD in front of my parents. At that time I was very private about my rituals and was embarrassed to acknowledge them. As we all sat in the small office room, Mr. Blumer pulled out a copy of my number chart used for washing. I immediately became uncomfortable since I kept these wash charts a secret. I had hand written several of these charts on paper to use and hid them. My mother must have taken one I had left around the house. Mr. Blumer then asked what they were used for. Since I was put on the spot I had no choice but to explain the method to my madness.

After speaking the awful truth my parents said nothing. I felt like I had just confessed to a crime. Notes were taken and silence filled the room. Mr. Blumer then discussed a recovery plan starting with subtle approaches to combat the OCD which would get more aggressive over time. A prescription for an antidepressant was written up. I was told it would increase the level of serotonin in my brain which could help with anxiety. That would be the first of very few visits I would make due to my lack of motivation at the time.

After graduation I continued to live with my parents. I had plans of going to a community college but decided to work for a while and save up some money to move out on my own. I worked most of the time while I was living there and built myself a nice little nest egg for when I left. Day-to-day living had its ups and downs. I had no rent to pay or food to buy but there were times when respect was needed from me which my OCD couldn't allow. These issues revolved around my washings in the house. I would need around 45 minutes to an hour in the shower. This amount of time gave me the ability to adequately wash particular areas of my body in my typical OCD fashion using my numbered chart. After the OCD requirements were met, I washed the rest of myself normally like anyone else would.

These extended showers would generally occur at night after work. I had a lot of closing shifts at the time which caused me to arrive home around 10:00 in the evening. My parents would be in bed at that time and were light sleepers. They slept in the upstairs loft which allows sounds to be heard very easily. As I would turn on the shower I would get nervous knowing there would be no way I could really cut down the wash time. My father was the lightest sleeper and if he awoke because of the shower running I was in big trouble. He would come to the shower and threaten to shut the water off if I did not shortly stop. There were very few times that I could stop when he wanted. It wasn't possible to comply without finishing these do-or-die tasks. When the water would shut off on me, I wrapped myself in a towel and lay in the living room until morning. When the water could be turned on again, I resumed.

As time passed, I slowly got closer to being independent. I desperately needed to do my OCD on my own terms. I needed the privacy and space to have uninterrupted washes. I had longed to have a place of my own for my OCD. It would be my secret hideout where my OCD could not be observed or stopped. I had acquired my own car and had savings to use. I was now waiting for the opportune time to depart and get a little more freedom from others. A new found love would soon blossom and kick start that process.

Chapter 4

My First Love

There have been several women that have come into my life over the years. I had always been successful with making a good first impression. I figured that part of it would be an important first step to finding a steady relationship. I put a lot of emphasis on my looks to overshadow my mental disabilities. During dates I would always be groomed and dressed to impress. I would act like I was an easy going kind of guy that enjoyed life. I also wanted to come across as being full of ambition to show I had a bright future ahead of me. I came up with a corny quote I used to say to girls. I would gaze at them intently and say, "The relationship KEY is that you become the WE and not the ME". That line alone either got a laugh or a sentimental smile, either way it got their attention in a positive way. Now you might think I was showing a false representation of myself, but I really wanted to be this imagined perfect person. My intentions were to be charming by putting my best foot forward in a manner of speaking. I had to work with what I could possibly offer and not what I actually had. Unfortunately, my OCD kept me from really becoming the man I was portraying. I knew if I was to have a shot with anybody I couldn't be upfront about my OCD in the beginning, it would have to slowly trickle in after an emotional connection had been established.

My first real relationship started at the age of 21 over the holidays while I was still living with my parents. I had been working for a department store when a coworker introduced me to Camille. She was a short petite looking blonde with an over eagerness to find the next "he's the one" guy. I was sucked in from the start, eager to find my first real relationship. Camille had worked in the same mall as I did. She was a barista for a coffee/deli shop. I broke the ice by giving her an invite only coupon to my department store along with a miniature size picture of myself complete with a written note on the back. The note included my cell number as well as my intent to ask her out.

After realizing I was interested in her, Camille and I soon developed a serious relationship. She herself had many relationships prior to me so she fit into her role very naturally. I on the other hand had to adjust to having a new girlfriend for the first time. There were adjustments that had to be made. I had to now combine my OCD and a relationship. The biggest hurdle was the hand holding. I had to make sure to have available times when my hands could be held. I didn't want to give Camille any indication I was scheduling this. She was clueless of my OCD at the time and didn't know that my hands had to be contaminant free to protect her. There were times when she wanted to show her affection by hand holding and I had to pull away. I'd always made up some type of reason why I couldn't hold her hand right in that very moment. My reasons were not always understandable to her due to their randomness at the time. Everything could be fine between us then I'd have to instantaneously find an excuse not to hold her hand as she would reach out for it. Awkwardness occurred as I began to panic in reaction to her. I tried to make up for these awkward moments by showing her more OCD friendly affection in replace of what I felt I couldn't do. Kissing was always fine with me since it did not involve hand touching. I became a very affectionate kisser for this reason.

Weeks turned into months, months turned into years with Camille. I was able to make it work by scheduling my own time alone for my OCD. I then made time for our relationship when I was free again. I was able to make this happen since we didn't live together which made it more manageable for me to separate the two. Eventually there was talk of moving in together. At that time, I could not have imagined life without her in it. My OCD would have to adapt somehow.

Camille had never lived with anyone before. She wanted to make sure we were going to take the next step by becoming engaged before we found a place together. I felt the time was right. She was my first love and I felt as strongly about her as I did my OCD. I moved into her parent's place and occupied her younger sister's empty room rent free for a couple of months. This gave me time to save for an engagement ring and have a little extra money for a deposit on a rental. Living there with my OCD was tolerable for those couple of months. If I had to wash my hands for an extended period of time, I did it in a lockable public bathroom away from her parent's home. My laundry was done at a laundromat where it could be washed in an OCD manner. My showers taken at her home and were between 30 - 40 minutes long. I took them when no one was home or her parents were busy doing tasks around the house in hopes of not drawing attention to myself. It worked for me for the duration of my stay there. I soon was engaged and living with Camille in a small two bedroom apartment a few miles away from her parent's home in Redmond.

At the time we moved in, I insisted that the extra room be used for a majority of my belongings. I sternly made it known that this room had to remain secure. Camille had no use for the room and seemed to respect my wishes. I didn't tell her but I could only enter the room if my hands were thoroughly washed, that way I could move items around and also add more if need be. If a major hand washing session had to take place, I made sure she was at work. I made sure to allocate private OCD obligated tasks behind her back. They mostly involved washing for hours. At times I felt as if I was keeping a deep dark secret from her.

Over time Camille began to have issues of her own. She was starting to think our life together wasn't good enough anymore. She started saying our place was depressing her due to the fact that we had little money to furnish it completely. She also kept telling me she was very unhappy and didn't know why when I would question her. Slowly she began having emotional highs and lows. The lows were more prevalent overall. I blame myself for some of it because I was withdrawn a lot when my OCD thoughts consumed me. She was eventually diagnosed with depression and bi-polar disorder. She would leave me at times and stay with her parents for comfort.

Eventually, her parents admitted her to a psychiatric facility in Portland, OR. This occurred near Thanksgiving and I was alone in the apartment now. She had taken all of her clothes but left her other belongings which give me hope she would return and we could continue our life together. She ended up remaining at the facility for about a month. Around Christmas her parent's called me and asked if I would like to accompany them to Portland to see her. I of course said yes! The trip there was quiet and I didn't realize until we arrived that Camille was not expecting me. When we arrived at the location her father Gary told me to remain in the waiting room while they checked up on her. About 10 minutes later her father gave me the go ahead to meet her. She was very surprised to say the least. It was a time of few words but high emotions. I kissed her forehead and massaged her back caringly. We, of course, said we loved each other as I left the building. I believe at the point we didn't know what kind of love we still had.

Camille left the facility soon after and remained at her parent's place. Christmas came and went without her spending it with me. It was hard for my family not to see her with me when I arrived Christmas Day to see them. The future seemed uncertain for her and I. Camille's parents thought it would be best for her to stay with them until she was more stable. I was not allowed to see her in person during this time. I would write her letters and drop them off. They would express how desperate I was to continue our relationship. According to her mother they would make her very upset causing her to cry uncontrollably, which abruptly ended my written communication with her.

Finally I received a call from her mother wanting to arrange a time to pick up the rest of her stuff. I knew from that moment on the relationship Camille and I had for 3 years was about to come to a close. What I thought was going to last forever had now seemed to have officially ended. I broke down over the phone questioning why this had to happen. At that point Gary got on the phone and threatened to come over with several men from his work if I did not cooperate. In shock, I immediately apologized and scheduled the following day for them to come by to get the rest of her belongings. That night I gathered everything she owned and placed it in the middle of the living room. The pile of belongings included her decorative knick-knacks and pillows, art pieces, blankets, and other items which made the apartment feel more inviting. They were all about to be gone along with her.

The next day her parents arrived. Out the window I could see their vehicle parked with them inside. Several minutes went by as they remained in the car. I assumed they must be discussing their plan of action. The doorbell rang and I let them in. They could see I had placed everything of Camille's out in the open for them. Not much was said as we loaded her stuff into her dad's truck. I was quick to head back after each load making sure no one was entering my secured room or snooping around. I was not hiding any of Camille's belongings but who's to say they weren't wondering. I felt compelled to at least open my secured room door so they could see there was nothing belonging to her inside. I was not about to let them do anything other than peak in. To my relief that was all that occurred. As soon as they left the apartment, I officially began to feel apart from the relationship. This event symbolized a complete separation from her. As a result of my first love leaving me, I soon fell into a great depression of my own.

The absence of her made me physically ill. My stomach felt as if it was in knots due to the tension my body was experiencing at the time. I was in no shape to do much so I took a few days off work and got prescribed a muscle relaxer to ease the physical pain. Trying to move on & stay positive proved to be much more difficult than I wanted. My life was about to take an unexpected turn for the worst which would alter my path ahead, giving me new direction.

Chapter 5

The Accident

I was now left alone to ponder things on my own. Camille and I had chosen this place together and it didn't feel right living there anymore. She had furnished most of the place so it was now practically empty except for our bed, hand-me-down couch, and television. My life now consisted of me, OCD, and a poor outlook. As I moped around the apartment, I began to think of an old saying I'd heard. It states that your first love is the hardest to get over. I couldn't have agreed more as I thought about my incomparable feelings I had towards Camille. Having that special someone to come home to everyday made me happy. Our relationship at times also gave me a much needed distraction from my own thoughts which I found beneficial. I obsessed less, thinking about us instead of always me. I didn't want to go back to my own personal problems alone. I had no choice but to accept that it was just going to be me again.

Getting up every day to go to work was a struggle since I didn't feel like I had much to live for. I would find myself oversleeping often so I wouldn't have to face my current situation. I woke up one very cold winter morning running late to work. I rushed to get dressed for another day at the department store. In a mild panic, I rushed to my Plymouth Neon and began my wintertime routine of ice scraping the car windshield. I always started up my engine while doing this to allow time for the vehicle to warm up as well. These tedious car preparations only wasted more of the time I didn't have that morning. Eventually, I was on the road driving towards the city of Bend where the mall was located. It was a 15 mile trip from where I lived in nearby Redmond. During that particular morning, the highway was iced over making driving condition more hazardous. While driving I had to slow for a more cautious driver ahead. I immediately became irritated, knowing this driver would only delay my work arrival even more. Without much thought or care for my own safety, I began to speed up to leave the driver behind me. As I entered the left lane to pass the vehicle I began to notice that I was now traveling on a thicker sheet of ice. This lane hadn't been used much this early in the morning and was very slick. My car began to sway as my wheels began to slide. I all of a sudden lost control of my car and began to spin. My vehicle made a 360 degree turn as it spun into oncoming traffic. My heart raced as I tried to regain control. I remember cars slamming on their brakes and sliding away from me. Then there was the one vehicle that could not avoid me. Everything happened so fast that by the time I felt an impact I had blacked out.

A dreadful awakening would be my next memory. I recall becoming conscious again as I was being physically shaken by a police officer checking my condition. My eyes opened as I sat in my now smashed-in car. Shattered glass lay all around me as I looked over my surroundings. I couldn't believe what had just happened to me. The officer asked me to try and move my all of my limbs. To my shock, I couldn't move my right arm at all. I began to panic, thinking if I could just wake that arm up and it would function again. The officer told me to remain calm. Soon after that was said, a helicopter had landed on the highway. I was carried out of the car and carefully strapped to a gurney. I vaguely remember the flight to the hospital as I tried to grasp the situation at hand. As I arrived at the hospital I was quickly given general anesthesia and was fast asleep.

I awoke to a cast on my right arm, IV in my vein, and a discomfort in my groin which I later found out was a catheter. I could not believe what I had gotten myself into. If only it could have all been a bad dream. What was supposed to have been a normal work day has now turned into a traumatic event I must face. I now had to adjust to my new aches and pains. My arm cast gave my hand limited mobility so hand washing would now be tricky. My parents were supportive through my entire stay. I ended up spending New Year's Eve in the hospital with them by my side. As we watched a movie together that night I felt very fortunate to have the family I did. They visited each day as I awaited doctor approval to leave.

Towards the end of my stay, Camille had gotten word of my accident from a mutual friend who worked at my department store. I started getting calls from her at the hospital asking to speak with me. Contact with her was the last thing I needed so I kept insisting that the hospital let her know not to call me there. This whole situation was emotionally draining enough without her making it worse. She kept pushing by calling several times a day. Eventually I gave in and she visited. She brought in pictures of us when she arrived which was completely unnecessary and hard to look at. What is she thinking? I thought to myself. Here I am injured and newly single and she has the nerve to want to reminisce. To shorten my aggravation with her I pretended to need sleep so she would go.

I stayed a total of 6 days in the hospital. I was ready to be discharged but the nurse assisting me was concerned that I hadn't had a bowel movement since the surgery. There was going to be no way I would even attempt to have one without my mittens available. I was not about to explain that at all to her, so I refused to try. Despite that concern, I eventually was able to leave. I was officially diagnosed as having a broken right arm, punctured lung, and minor fractures in the spine. I feel very fortunate to have been told I would be able to make a full recovery.

Compiled from Bulletin staff reports

Bend man injured on Highway 97

A 24-year-old Bend man was in stable condition Wednesday afternoon after his vehicle slid into oncoming traffic on Highway 97 earlier in the day.

Derek Ferris was transported by Air Life to St. Charles Medical Center-Bend after the accident.

According to the Deschutes County Sheriff's Office, Ferris was headed south when he lost control of his Plymouth Neon on the slick roadway near The Brand restaurant. The vehicle slid into the northbound lane and was struck on the passenger side by a Dodge Intrepid driven by Max Bliven, 31, of Redmond.

Both vehicles were towed from the scene with major damage but no other injuries were reported.

The highway was closed briefly so that Air Life was able to land.

Sgt. Michael Johnston of the Sheriff's Office would like motorists to be particularly aware of road conditions this time of year, urging drivers to "slow down and use caution."

No citations were issued and the accident is still under investigation.

Article from Bend Bulletin Newspaper

33

Chapter 6

On My Own

After I recovered from my accident I was about ready to be on my own. I had been living with my parents through winter, spring, and most of summer. My OCD had to be minimized during this period so I could heal. Having a broken arm and minor spine injuries made it difficult to do much at first. My left hand had to now do what the right couldn't. My cast also had to be wrapped in plastic during showers. My parent's at this point have had enough experience dealing with me and my OCD. Due to my circumstances my mother was more accommodating to me and my preferences while I was there. She knew I needed deposable gloves for certain tasks and she without question made sure I could purchase them.

My father helped me get back on my feet by offering to cover half of the cost for another car. He and I traveled to Portland in search of my new car. We checked out many dealerships with lots of options. A new car of mine would be considered an expensive procession and therefore would require certain cleanliness standards. My Dad kept getting into the cars I was considering. He would sit in the driver's seat, touch the steering wheel and check the dash board functions. There was no way I was going to allow that to happen to the car I was choosing to take back home. I was too embarrassed to specifically ask him to stop. Luckily for me my body language and unwillingness to let him in specific cars eventually gave him the message. It took a while but finally at the end of the day, I choose a nicely kept 2000 Chevy Tracker 4X4 that my Dad only checked the oil in. I figured I could live with that! I then followed my Dad back over the mountains in my new car until we reached home.

Shortly after acquiring my vehicle I had nothing holding me back from moving. I wanted a fresh start somewhere new. The high desert climate of Central Oregon with its frigid winters was no longer appealing. The more populated Willamette Valley to the west would be milder for me. It was a two and half hour drive away over the mountains. I was interested in the city of Eugene on the south end. It was a classic college town with an arts vibe. A coworker from my department store in Bend was going to attend The University of Oregon there in the fall and wanted a 4th roommate to live in a quad apartment complex complete with furnishings, private bathrooms, and mini fridges. I thought this would be the perfect setup for me! I promptly submitted a transfer request to through my department store to work in that location. I was soon approved and all ready to go once the quad room was available. I was excited to have a job and place to live waiting for me. I packed up my clothes and loaded them into my vehicle. My parents waved goodbye as I drove off to once again find independence on my own.

The quad room in Eugene was small. It came with a twin bed, wardrobe cabinet, and the mini fridge that was about half of what a full sized fridge would be. The private bathroom and shower were acceptable for what I needed them for. The kitchen section connected all four rooms and would have to be shared. I hardly knew the one coworker whom I would be sharing it with. His two other friends who were also University students would be occupying the two other rooms. This was going to be my new home and I was going to make the best of it.

Shortly after moving in and being introduced to everyone in the quad things changed rapidly. The three other roommates who hadn't seen the rooms prior to moving in decided all a sudden to move out together. They forfeited their deposits and quickly left. I was told the living conditions didn't meet their expectations. They all offered me the chance to move into a rental home with them but I declined. I was not about to share more than I had to with people otherwise it would not work out.

I never kept in touch with any of the guys after their departure. The other three rooms of the quad had now become available to anyone who wanted to rent the space. I had no idea when or who would occupy the rooms. I had no real friends here so I welcomed the idea of having new renters.

Many interesting characters came and went over the next two years I spent there. Some only stayed a few months; others were exchange students who stayed through the entire school year. When I wanted to be social I would hang out in the kitchen area, otherwise I would keep to myself in the privacy of my room. I never allowed anyone in my room with the exception of one instance involving a one night stand.

Living in a college town was fun and when my OCD was under control I enjoyed it. During the weekends I would dress to impress and experience the nightlife. One particular night I met a girl at a dance club and we had a drink together. She arrived there with her friend who seemed to have found a man of her own. After chatting for a while as a group she then gave her friend the go ahead to leave. It was just the two of us now. We had a psychical connection established between us at this point. It was getting late and I told her I would walk her back to her car which was near my quad.

We got to her car and I was about to say goodnight when she grabbed me and we began to kiss. Her back lay against the car as I purposely brushed up against her. I could tell she was really into it. I then asked what we do from here. She whispered into my ear and said "we're both adults and you know what I want". I realized she wanted to spend the night with me. I was torn at that moment because I really wanted this to happen but my OCD was telling me no! I had to overcome my hesitance and push myself if I was going to allow this to occur at my place. I knew this was a rare situation for me and I, being a young man, couldn't resist.

She followed me to my quad and I let her in. Fortunately for me, we did nothing other than get right to it. Afterwards we both instantly fell asleep in my cramped twin bed. The morning after was stressful because I didn't want anything to happen that I didn't approve. She wanted to use the bathroom so I had to think quickly. My place was small and I feared my clean bathroom faucet could be accidentally splashed with water from the contaminated sink I washed in. I remembered the quad next to me was unoccupied as well as unlocked so I escorted her to the bathroom there. I made up a cover story about how my bathroom was being remodeled currently. My scheme was convincing enough due to my bathroom door being closed. I may have had to appease my OCD, but I still shared my place with someone.

Soon after we hugged one last time and she left. I was quite proud of myself and not just because I had sex with her. The whole experience represented that I could let my guard down in an effort to not miss out. I just needed more motivators other than getting laid to realize it.

Skinner Butte
Eugene, OR

Chapter 7

Three Worlds

After being on my own for a while I needed to figure out a way to minimize the constant switching from clean to dirty and dirty to clean. I decided to create three worlds for myself; one clean, one clean enough, and one dirty. My clean world is where I am most comfortable. In this world I, as well as my surroundings, am clean. There is never any worry of contamination because nothing has come into contact with anything I would be concerned with. In this type of situation my OCD does not exist. It's as if I never had it. I am able to live freely in this world. I am able to touch, feel, and experience anything in this type of setting. It's a world that is created anytime I go to a place I have kept clean or travel to an unvisited location where no known contamination has taken place.

My clean-enough-world was created to allow me the ability to have a better relationship going forth with any women I would later pursue. Before this third world was created there was only a clean and dirty world. The clean-enough-world was a must if I was going to have a successful relationship with anyone. It's a complicated world that's not as black and white. It requires that the partner follow some annoying but tolerable rules my OCD must have. They do the minimum for my OCD to keep me from constant anxiety. This request, once a relationship has gotten serious, has never been easy to insist. I have always felt extremely embarrassed and ashamed once these needs are addressed. I am emotionally distressed with concern at that point. My results have been positive for the most part due to the fact that I care and am sincere with my words.

My contaminated world is extremely filthy to me. I avoid this world whenever I can, but will stay in it as long as I have to. There is an instant understanding from within myself that I will have to exhaustively complete a thorough washing if I am ever to return to my other two worlds. My clothes, which are used as a protective layer in this world, must be carefully removed and washed as well. I only use thicker clothing in this world which has to completely cover my arms and legs. When contaminated, I can move freely about my dirty world and touch and do anything, since everything in it is already contaminated. Nothing in it has to be cleaned or avoided.

These three worlds exist side-by-side like parallel universes that are never allowed to meet. This is my reality and how my OCD deals with my environments. I try to make the most of my time while in each world. I will set aside tasks or activities to do while in each one. My clean world involves duties that include moving, buying, and replacing items that have been kept clean. This world is also utilized when receiving services like haircuts, doctor, or dental visits that involve touching. My clean-enough-world includes couple activities were we follow minimal OCD rules and share things such as household appliances, food, computer, TV, etc. This world is in a grey area which changes over time as I try to adapt by incorporating less OCD than I did. The dirty world duties can include trash removal, floor scrubbing, or interactions with people that I consider contaminated.

It is too complicated for my mind not to separate the world this way. I have to be able to set expectations in most of my everyday situations. A mix of conditions that I am not prepared for has proven to be disastrous for my OCD. There is always a risk of uncertainty, but staying on top of things to the best of my ability has only relieved me of anxiety. It's about being the best I can be with OCD.

Chapter 8

The Family Effect
Part 1

Coming to terms with the lifestyle of my immediate family has been very difficult to overcome. Over the years, I've witnessed too many concerning issues which have put my OCD into panic mode whenever I am around them. It wasn't always as intense for me, but overtime, as my parents acquired property in the country complete with horses, dogs, cats, and chickens, it got worse. Witnessing animal waste outside and the certainty of knowing traces have made their way onto the floors of their home have caused constant anxiety for me. The anxieties would peak as I began to notice hand and body contact with the floors. This situation unfortunately grew in scale and consumed me. An OCD-fueled avoidance had started between me and the family I love causing many challenges for me.

The realization of the importance family has on one's life is the motivator for me to find ways around my issues. My love for them is unconditional therefore must prevail somehow, some way. My methods of coping have not always been healthy but are effective. They include more covered clothing and throw away or washable items brought while visiting. A sleeping bag along with pillows are brought during an overnight stay and placed over any bed used.

A decontamination process is initiated immediately after returning home which includes the removal of all clothes worn as well as OCD washes to any affected areas that were not covered. This type of recovery process can vary depending on how careful I was during the visit.

Gifts definitely play a part with family. Anything given to me by them has to be OCD friendly or I unfortunately have no use for it due to its contamination. This harsh understanding that I needed to have was not easy to make known. If not careful enough my intentions could easily be misconstrued as unappreciative or hurtful if I ever decided to be upfront with this concern. An OCD friendly gift can be many things as long as it is something that can't be touched from the inside, is used only temporary, or can be washed. Anything protected in an unopened box, a gift card, or washable clothing works just fine. It was soon assumed that I had some type of reasoning behind my consistent preferences when asked for birthday or Christmas gift ideas. If something was odd with me they knew to associate it with my OCD. I had to give them clarity on the matter eventually after a few unwanted gifts were given. It wasn't right of me to risk having them purchase something I would later throw away. As upsetting as it was to comprehend my needs, there still had to be a mutual understanding that I still cared about their feelings and was grateful for what they did for me out of love.

The one thing I promised myself I could never do to my family would be to take things way too far. I don't ever want to present myself as being completely protected from them. It would cut down on the washing dramatically. I could wear gloves and surrender to my OCD during visits. I don't because I know my family deserves better. I care what they think of me as a son, brother, and uncle. Otherwise, I would show up on the doorstep in a space suit! In all honesty they all have a place in my heart and I will continue to battle my OCD in an effort to spend more time with them.

My Parent's Place

Chapter 9

Purchase Predicaments

My OCD has a way of always needing more from the store. I have spent years analyzing what types of products protect and clean best through trial and error. I have narrowed it down to five must have items to purchase on a regular basis. They include a constant supply of liquid hand soap, foam soap, garbage bags, antibacterial wet wipes, and nitrile deposable gloves. With these supplies, I am best equipped to universally function in the demanding world I create. They will get me back to my clean self after I've come in contact with anything considered contaminated.

The liquid soap washes away contamination from the flatter surfaces of my hand or item being cleaned. The foam soap reaches areas in between my fingers or crevices needing to be washed. The garbage bags and wet wipes are vital for scrubbing and restroom use. Finally, the nitrile disposable gloves are needed to provide a more flexible barrier and grip for carefully handled tasks. I try to always buy in bulk and stock up on these mandatory supplies. Running out of these specific items during a task in progress has proven countless times to abruptly halt my ability to continue.

These rare occasions result in a desperate attempt to inconveniently purchase more. I usually have no extra time in these circumstances. I have run late to work, family gatherings, and obligated events during these last minute trips to the store, (the most embarrassing of which being walking into my grandma's funeral in progress). I have to make up excuses for my tardiness every time. Openly saying it was my OCD's fault is just not acceptable even though it is the truth.

Desperate purchase attempts made for my OCD have included stealing from stores at times. Being on my own meant I had to balance my living expenses with my OCD expenses. I had to learn to be responsible with money while maintaining my OCD. Living alone and excessively buying OCD supplies dwindled my funds so I couldn't buy what I needed. I had to occasionally resort to shoplifting. I couldn't just do without because it affected my ability to properly function. I would be crippled with anxiety unless I did what I had to for the OCD side of me.

Garbage bags would end up being my most frequently shoplifted item. Being in large boxes they were not easy to conceal. I had to quickly walk in and walked out of the store when I thought the coast was clear. Eventually I had a close call as a result of my behaviors. It occurred at night while I was concealing some soap in my jacket pocket at a nearby grocery store. I decided to pay for some additional items so I didn't look suspicious. I had stolen from this store before so security must have been on to me. The line was long as I waited to pay. I could see the security guard near the exit eyeballing everyone. I got nervous knowing I could be caught. It was now my turn to pay for my items and get out of there. As I approached the exit I passed the security guard. He was an elderly man who intently glared at me as I left. Just as I walked out of the store a police car pulled up next to me. An officer got out and proceeded to walk into the store paying no attention to me. As he entered the store I ran out into the dark streets and hid a few blocks away. Within minutes of my getaway that same police car with its lights now on drove right past me as I quietly sat in the bushes near the road. I knew the police must have arrived for me, otherwise why did they leave promptly after I did. They must have been called in and just missed me. The experience added unnecessary paranoia to my already heightened anxiety. I would have to be more disciplined with my expenses from now on. I didn't need to include being a thief in my life anymore. I never stole again!

Despite my harrowing ordeals, I have had successful purchasing experiences. I am a big fan of the U-Scan; a machine used to purchase items without the use of a cashier. The U-Scan is a way for me to ring up my own purchases. It allows me the ability to be the only one who is touching my merchandise. I make the majority of my purchases at Walmart, Fred Meyer, Albertsons, and Home Depot because they have U-Scan available. When my hands are clean, ringing up my own purchases is easy. When I feel my hands are contaminated, I make use of other merchandise in the store to pick up what I need. Tongs for example, are useful for moving items from the shelves to the cart and finally to the U-Scan. When I'm done using my alternative hands, I leave these items unpurchased at the checkout. I most certainly look weird at times but this method does the job I need it to do. There have been instances where store security has been called to observe my behaviors. These occasions make for a very uncomfortable experience when no harm has been done.

I will occasionally let a checker ring my purchases up if they are assumed to be contamination free. I generally have to be at a store I have never been in before for this to happen. This is the case because I have not witnessed any contamination there. When contamination at a store occurs it is when items are being dropped to the floor by customers on accident, or kids are being placed in shopping carts with their dirty shoes on.

Another way I purchase clean items is by ordering them online, mostly from Amazon because of the wide variety of items they carry. This gives me access to products which are protected in a box and delivered straight to my door. If I am not home, I leave a note for the delivery man to place the box in a tub which I leave by the door. The tub keeps the box from being placed on the dirty ground. This process for purchasing items has always worked well when I didn't need something immediately.

Chapter 10

Job Issues

Everyone has to make a living somehow and for me it's been a struggle to achieve this having OCD. I am generally able to keep a job for a couple of years at a time but things have a way of eventually not working out in most cases. However, moving out on my own and having more control of my OCD has helped prolong my jobs.

Prior to my transfer to Eugene, everything worked fairly well with the department store I worked for with one exception. I had to wash one section of my hands using my numbered chart prior to actually working. This one section included the palm side of my right and left hand fingers which always had contaminants left on them from living with my parent's at the time. Washing had to be done at the department store because I felt the bathroom faucets were cleaner there. In my mind, I didn't want to risk transferring anything to the store. The store had to remain contamination free to insure the public as well as the clothes I frequently bought from there were clean. This type of OCD friendly work environment I was trying to maintain kept me satisfied and focused on customer service.

Getting out the door, driving to work, and setting aside 5 quite non-interrupted minutes in a public bathroom caused frequent problems for me. This resulted in continual tardiness, which eventually got noticed and brought to my attention multiple times by management and department staff. I did the best I could do by trying to allow ample time before starting work.

I knew things were getting out of hand when I was followed one time into the store's bathroom by security. I proceeded to wash with my chart out when the undercover security guard entered. The store hired private security and the man knew me well. He went directly to the sink next to me pretending to wash his hands without soap, waiting to see what I would do next. I was hoping he would stop and leave me alone. He didn't so I had to stop and walk out. I felt as if he was warning me that this was unacceptable here. Shortly after the encounter, I was able to find another more isolated bathroom out in the mall where I could continue.

After I moved to Eugene other issues occurred at work. They slowly began after I was placed in the shoe department. Having floor contamination issues and working where customers place most everything on the floor was a bad situation for me to be in. I was under constant threat of being consumed by my OCD. I could, at any moment, be handicapped with fear.

I began noticing repeat customers from outside of work walking in known contamination areas throughout town. They would then later on visit my department to try on shoes. These unfortunate observations lead to the entire store floor being contaminated in my eyes. Since floor usage is vital to selling shoes, my OCD was in big trouble. I was always confronting my fears as I watched customers place their hands on the bottoms of shoes after trying them on. The aggravation continued as I constantly picked up the shoe boxes off the floor. This led to excessively long breaks to wash my hands. My coworkers began to notice that I would just disappear all a sudden throughout the day. I eventually was given a verbal warning which led to multiple write-ups threatening disciplinary action. It all got to be too much for me and I was fired.

My next job had to be nothing like the last so I applied for a call center position where I could remain seated and off the floor. The interview went well and I was soon hired. I handled incoming customer service calls for a major cellular phone company and enjoyed it. The job seemed to be working out. I had what I thought was my own cubicle, headset, and computer. Little did I know that I was about to find out otherwise.

After discovering that the lower level men's restroom had a private locker room I quickly acquired a locker to place my jacket, cell phone and snacks in. I made a stop there before every shift, and before leaving to go home. One day as I was headed home, I noticed a paper note placed on the restroom door which led to the locker room. The note said "Restroom closed for cleaning". I had to enter to reach my locker. As I approached the locker room I was in a state of shock and disbelief at what I was looking at. Instant anxiety hit me like a punch in the face. The entire locker room floor was covered in what appeared to be toilet waste. I was looking at a wet floor with toilet paper and feces scattered all about. What was the cause of this horrific and unforgettable sight in front of me? I soon realized there must have been a septic system clog which affected the adjacent showers causing the toilet waste to back up and flow out from the drains. I had to reach my locker, so I carefully stepped around the solid pieces of waste below me. I was relieved to find out the inside of my locker was dry. I quickly left in panic mode. I was full of disgust, anxiety, and bitterness knowing the mental damage this would now create for me here.

I knew from that point on, the contamination from that floor would spread traces throughout the entire building. This event kept me focused on the floors at all times while I was working there. I began to notice coworkers dropping things like paper, pens, and coins to the floor and picking them up. Now anything these coworkers touched with their hands was going to be contaminated as well. This would include door handles, time clock punch buttons, keyboards, etc. It was then obvious to assume these traces were going to spread like wild fire and affect everyone. My heightened observations lead to me noticing that my cubicle had been used on my days off. After questioning the cause, I found out the new hires in training could use unoccupied cubicles even though they were assigned. This lead to my headset being used which I was not about to then put back on my head.

I knew I couldn't successfully wash the headset in the manner I needed to without hours of aggravation involved. I also had no guarantee that washing it wouldn't cause damage to the headset. I had no choice but to take time off until I could somehow get ahold of a new headset. I thought I could just pick up a new one at a nearby electronics store and everything would be fine. I knew everything else at work would only affect my hands which could then be washed. The headset was the only issue I had to resolve and it had to be done by purchasing a new one. To my frustration I found out the headset needed was an expensive specialty product that had to be ordered online. After spending around $85.00 and waiting three business days I received my headset.

When not in use I kept the headset in my locker to protect it. My hands were always contaminated at work which made putting the headset on tricky. I would always touch the extended microphone piece and carefully lift the headset onto and off of my head every day.

I wasn't always successful in getting the headset on and off without contamination from my hands either touching my head or additional parts of the headset. In an effort to keep my job I tried to cope with my anxiety if small areas where contaminated that I could fix. Once the small areas got to be larger areas it was too much for me to handle. My OCD had to get its way or my job performance would ultimately suffer as a result. I was determined to make this job work so I ordered more expensive headsets to replace the old ones every few months as needed. Eventually the expenses involved and the washes endured were not going to make the call center job tolerable anymore. I resigned and was once again unemployed.

What could I possibly do next? I had now become distraught over my circumstances. My OCD could now be relieved to some extent but I had traded one problem for another through losing my income. I thought maybe I should apply for disability benefits through social security. However, if I did that I'm basically giving up on myself. I didn't want to let the OCD win by receiving assistance. I knew I could do better by keeping faith in my potential. I was fully capable of something and I was going to keep searching.

Chapter 11

State Of Being

I have always been captivated by the idea of being carefree. I had always associated it with happiness. How wonderful it must be to experience extended periods where you can be free of worry, concern, and unwanted responsibility. In today's world it can be more of a privilege to feel this way. Now if you take the world we live in, add OCD into it, you now have a stressfully enhanced version of modern day-to-day living. Trying to manage my OCD was all I could handle dealing with, any extra problems on the side proved to be too much for me at times. Everything else in my personal life needed to run smoothly or else despair would be inevitable. During my unemployment periods I would seek temporary relief by drinking alcohol excessively. Living near the university provided me with plenty of nightclubs and bars all within walking distance of where I lived. I had made friends with a new quad neighbor next door named Nathan. He was an exchange student from Haiti who introduced me to some of his other friends when they would come over to visit. Nathan, like most students, would party on the weekends. One Saturday night proved to be a major wake up call for me.

It started while at a get-together taking place at a high rise apartment in downtown Eugene. The apartment was rented out by a friend of Nathan. This friend had traveled to many countries and was very cultured. He had a passion for anything fun and spontaneous. He loved to drink and enticed me to drink along with him prior to us going to a dance club afterwards.

I then proceeded to drink two bottles of red wine over the course of one hour. I had never been overly intoxicated so I did not know my limits. After all the wine had been consumed those carefree feelings were beginning to kick in. I was enjoying being in the moment at last. My body felt light and my emotions were only joyous. My reality sober had drifted from me. I didn't want to let this feeling fade away.

The next hour was great and I had forgotten my problems completely. We arrived at the nightclub looking for women to add to our enjoyment. The club was dark with flashing lights, beams, and lasers which caused disorientation. Within the next few minutes I began to experience dizziness. I had the sense that my surroundings were spinning. My vertigo intensified to a point where I was unable to walk. I sat curled up against a wall and closed my eyes. My condition was soon noticed by security and I was escorted outside. I sat on the street curb while the security guard reached for my phone. I was vomiting heavily as he began asking if he could call somebody for me. I handed over my phone and had him call the first name that popped into my head, which was a guy by the name of Jeremiah, who I knew had a car. Jeremiah was more of an acquaintance than a friend. He had been introduced to me by Nathan and would be reliable.

Jeremiah was quick to pick me up in his beat-up station wagon. He helped me into his car and took off to the hospital. As we arrived we entered the emergency room. Jeremiah placed me in a wheeled chair and assisted in discussing my condition. He made sure I was taken care of before leaving. The rest of my night was forgotten.

I woke up the next morning in a hospital gown with fluids intravenously being given through a vein in my arm. This was administered to fight dehydration. I felt recovered but weak. As I awoke to this embarrassment before me, the nurse handed me a box where my clothes had been placed. As I put them back on, I noticed they were damp and disgustedly smelled of vomit. I was mortified at the thought of what happened. I walked the quiet streets that Sunday morning back to my quad with an awakened sense of responsibility for my own actions.

Was I expecting to find some sort of peace through drinking? If I did, it would lead to more problems. I had the perfect example fresh in my mind from last night. I knew if I was going to have a more anxiety free life I would have to be under the influence of something healthier. My focus now shifted to the importance of regularly taking my prescription drugs. The lack of motivation to take them over the years had been for two reasons: the side effects and required doctor visits to receive more. They were bothersome enough that I didn't put the emphasis I should of on it. My excuses seemed irrelevant now.

As a result of having OCD I was really good at obsessing about anything I wanted to place focus on. Obsessing was a frame of mind that was only beneficial when analyzing what created positivity for me. I came to an understanding within myself that I was fixated on what needed to be and not what was. I had become dependent on particular outcomes as I progressed in life. Changes I felt I needed couldn't, in most cases, happen overnight. I had to be satisfied to some extent with the here and now. Thankfulness has become a big part of how I combat my feelings of inadequacy. Knowing things could always be worse and showing appreciation for the better parts of my life was crucial. The perfectionist side of me was able to be put more at rest as I gained this new found capability. What is considered perfect may never fully be achieved to the extent I wanted it and my expectations had to be rationalized better.

With the financial help of my parents I once again visited the doctor. I was put on different medication in hopes of it having fewer side effects. I was getting back on track with a more hopeful outlook. Over time, that cheerful feeling you have when nothing is troubling you slowly became more apparent in my life.

Chapter 12

An Unexpected Friend

Having my kind of OCD makes it hard to maintain friendships for long periods of time. It is easy for me to act likable but my OCD eventually gets in the way. When there has been time for it, I have made friends but I have to allow it to happen and my OCD needs to be under control. There has been one time when a friendship developed unexpectedly when I wasn't looking for it. It began after I moved into my first studio apartment in Eugene. I lived in a tiny 1 room, 1 bath with kitchenette apartment. After living there a few months a new tenant arrived. He moved into an upstairs apartment. His name was James and he had a peculiar personality. One day he came up to me and asked if I had a dollar bill. I checked my wallet and asked what he needed it for.

"I don't need a dollar; just wanna know if you have one," he said.

I looked at him with confusion and said, "So why would you be asking for money if you don't need any?"

He replied, "I'm just asking." I looked into my wallet just to humor him.

"Nope, sorry," I said. He then proceeded to take a one dollar bill out of his wallet.

"I want to show you something," he said. He began intricately folding the dollar bill, making sure every bend was precise. A minute or two went by as I watched him. The dollar had transformed from a flat one dimensional object into a sculpted bird through his folding technique. I instantly realized he practiced the art of paper folding known as origami. James proudly handed me his finished product. At that moment, I realized he wanted to surprise me by not saying too much. His method in doing so was odd, but I felt harmlessness from him.

James was new to Eugene and was attending The University of Oregon pursuing a major in music. He played a brass valve instrument called a euphonium, which resembled a small tuba. I could tell he placed a lot of emphasis on his talents to overshadow his obvious weaknesses, which I couldn't quite put my finger on just yet. He soon revealed to me that he had Asperger Syndrome. This disorder is considered a high-functioning form of autism which can cause difficulty interacting socially. I now understood what was behind his awkward ways.

As the months passed, James grew on me. I respected his drive to make friends despite his difficulties in doing so. His social skills always needed work but the guy meant well. He expressed to me his desire to find a girlfriend and eventually start a relationship. He had no preferences on the type of girl he was looking for. He just wanted a female companion to accept and love him. He would have to find someone special, a possible difficult task; nonetheless he was going to try.

Whenever he wasn't in class, it felt like he'd be in his apartment waiting for me to come home. He would usually leave his door open so he or I would know each other was there. He was always exited to see me as I arrived home from work.

In my free time we hung out together. I took it upon myself to help him with his appearance and social behaviors. I took him shopping and picked out some trendy clothes for him to wear. He was a bigger guy so we had to find just the right fit for him. I also assisted with his grooming habits. I showed him how to style his hair and maintain his beard perfectly using a trimmer. He soon mastered everything I had showed him which gave him new found confidence in what he could become.

Now that James had a new improved look it was time to go out and practice his social skills with me by his side. Since he was so talented at dollar bill origami I figured the most fun we could have together would be at a strip club! I knew he could impress the girls with his skills every time he gave them money. James had never been to a strip club so this would be an unforgettable experience and maybe an ego boost if he got attention.

Friday approached and we were ready to start the night off right. James premade several dollar bill animals for us both to give out. He would be able to show off what he could do making me look good along with him. We arrived at the Silver Dollar Strip Club full of anticipation for what awaited us. We found a seat, ordered drinks and pulled out James's creatively folding dollars. We waited eagerly for each girl on stage to react to our uniqueness. To our delight it sparked a conversation after every pole dance. We stood out in the crowd and James loved every minute of it.

"How did you do that?" they would ask. I gave James credit for his talents as he proudly discussed his abilities with them. His tiny works of art were seen as cute and we took full of advantage of the attention. We gave out our entire pile of dollar animals and made a good impression. As we left I could tell James felt a sense of worth, validation, and praise from the girls on stage. I was happy to have helped build his confidence. His social insecurities with women had now been put more at ease.

The two of us would usually spend weekends together. One particularly memorable night we showed up late to a dance club in downtown Eugene. The club was packed full. There was about an hour left before close. Most of the people inside drinking alcohol had reached their peak intoxication level by now. James and I stood and watched the spectacle in front of us. The dance floor was alive with people doing a combination of what I'd call drunk and dirty dancing. They'd hold their drinks in one hand and try to sexually engage in some type of dance which mostly involved rubbing themselves on one another. It looked fun if you weren't sober. After a few minutes of visual entertainment, a Hispanic woman approached me.

"Do you want to dance?" she asked. She was probably in her late thirties and I didn't find her attractive.

"No thanks" I said. At that moment I knew James could take my place. Without another word I immediately grabbed him from behind me and said, "This guy will!"

I figured this would be another perfect opportunity for James to get some more experience with the opposite sex. The woman accepted and James took her to the dance floor. The dirty song "Play" by David Banner started. This particular song was very explicit and James memorized every word in it. As they slow danced he proceeded to quietly whisper the lyrics of the song into her ear as if it was meant for her. I was very impressed by his attempt to seduce this woman.

After the song ended, the lights in the club turned on and it was closing time. I left the club and told James I would wait for him outside. A couple of minutes later James came running out of the club. He was filled with excitement as he told me that this woman wanted to go home with him. James had only one concern. His apartment was a mess and he needed me to clean it up a little before he showed up with her. He gave me his keys and I quickly had to make the 15 minute walk back in time before they both would arrive in her car. By the time I got to our apartments, James had just pulled in and was waiting in her car. James watched me rush to his apartment door. When I got inside, I frantically began picking up his scattered papers, magazines, and food. Meanwhile James was trying to stall her as they got out of her car. They started walking up the stairs while I was finishing up. I had his apartment door wide open. James knew I was still in his apartment. He grabbed the woman's arm and held her back as she tried going further up the stairs.

"You're not going to rape me are you?" she asked. James let her go and she made her way to the top of the stairs. She looked at me as I walked out of James's apartment. I couldn't help laughing as I walked downstairs to my studio. I was embarrassed for him but at the same time hopeful.

The next morning I looked out my window and noticed her car still remained outside. I knew without a doubt that James successfully had his first one night stand! I felt a little bad knowing the encounter would more than likely not develop into any kind of lasting relationship. I, of course, asked him later how everything went and he kept on saying thank you!

Our adventures while single brought James and I closer together. He felt like a younger brother and he looked up to me like one. I eventually opened up about having OCD. He didn't give it much thought and went along with whatever preferences I had while we were together. He valued our friendship and that was all that mattered to him. James rarely ever questioned me and that was just the way I liked it. James was a more OCD tolerable person to be around. He required patience but so did I. He gave me unconditional acceptance and was always forgiving for my faults. We both had our issues, they were just different. Overall the friendship made me a more accepting person to others. I began to realize that a disability can come in many forms and to overlook what might be thought at first. I came to the conclusion that everyone has potential no matter what may hold them back.

James & I in 2008

Chapter 13

The Relationship Trials

When my OCD was under control and I had spare time I would get online and the use social networking service MYSPACE. I had created a profile account were I would now and then search for women in my area to chat with. My account had my most flattering pictures available to view on it which I hoped would attract the opposite sex. It was like fishing hoping you get a bite. The majority of my efforts resulted in a lot of causal dating which emptied my wallet fairly quickly. There were, however, a few memorable short term relationships that did develop.

The first was named Jeannine who contacted me with a flirty line to break the ice. She was a recently turned brunette whose new hair color from blonde represented her attempt at a fresh start with a new appearance. We set up a dinner date at the Olive Garden to meet. As I arrived at the restaurant, I received a phone call. It was her canceling and wanting to reschedule for some unknown reason. She seemed sincere about still wanting to meet up, so we planned on a later time.

The second time around she was at the restaurant early waiting for me which made up for the prior cancelation. We had dinner and drinks while she discussed her recent breakup and need to move on. I played the good listener showing sympathy and understanding. She was very attractive and I began to overlook the fact she may be going from one relationship to the next right away to avoid the pain of the breakup.

She mentioned to me she had a roommate named Braxton who she was living with. Braxton was also single and looking to date someone. Without giving it much thought I arranged a second double date were I would introduce James to Braxton in hopes he would either find a girl of his own or just get laid. The night of our double date started off exciting. I made sure James was dressed to impress. He had his hair styled, cologne lightly sprayed on, and a fashionable outfit. We were ready to go! Before we arrived I stressed to him the importance of being aware of his social awkwardness and making a good first impression. I wanted this to be as much of a success for me and it could be for him if he played his cards right.

We walked in and got a table. Soon the girls walked in and found us. Jeannine sat across from me while Braxton sat across from James. I could tell my talk with James made him extremely nervous and quite. He didn't want to screw this up and say something wrong. My conversation flow with Jeannine went fine, yet James was having problems opening up to Braxton. She did most of the talking while James made very few comments. We ate as I tried including all of us in conversation. Braxton finally asked if there was something wrong with him. James froze with hesitation as he looked at her. I finally had to step in and say quietly that he had Asperger Syndrome. At that point things got awkward and the girls went to the bathroom. I looked at him with a disappointed expression.

"You screwed up buddy," I said as I looked over the check. I was very frustrated with him for messing up this perfectly good opportunity. The girls came back and were ready to go. James sat in shame by himself as I escorted them outside.

"Do you have any friends that aren't weird?" Braxton asked.

I replied, "Yes!" and apologized for James's behavior. The girls then let me know that they wanted to continue the evening, just not with James. I told them I completely understood and would try to contact someone else for Braxton so we could all hang out later that night.

The truth is I knew no one else at the time. I didn't want to come across as having no other friends so I called Jeannine and said none of my other friends were available. Braxton ended up inviting a male coworker over to their home that night. I was then given the go ahead to come over. I left my apartment complex annoyed with James for delaying my time with Jeannine. James spent the rest of the evening alone in his apartment depressed.
I drove quickly to their home, not wanting to waste any more time.

When I arrived, the four of us drank and I was introduced to Hookah smoking. Hookahs are water pipes that are used to smoke specially made tobacco that comes in different flavors. The hookah used had multiple hoses connected to the main pipe so we could all smoke from our own hose which had a mouth piece attached to the end. My OCD was put more at ease knowing we would not all be sharing one. The alcohol and smoking started to put everyone at ease with one another. Pictures were taken of Jeannine and I being affectionate, having fun and goofing off.

As the night came to a close, there seemed to be an expectation that the coworker and I would be staying the night. Braxton took him to her room while Jeannine took me to her's. I sat down on her bed. Jeannine left to use the bathroom. A couple of minutes later she returned completely naked. I was in shock at that moment. I had only been on 2 dates with her and there she was giving herself to me. I immediately got up, looking her up and down in the process. All I could think to say was "You're beautiful" and we began to kiss. I moved her over to the bed and began removing my clothes.

We were just about ready to have sex when she all of a sudden said, "I can't do this". She then went back to the bathroom. I became confused and frustrated as I put back on my clothes. I was about to leave when Braxton came out of her room asking what I was doing. I told her that I didn't think Jeannine would need me anymore tonight. Braxton insisted I stay till morning. She entered the bathroom Jeannine was in and asked her if I should stay. Braxton then came out to let me know Jeannine wanted me to stay. I headed back to her bedroom. Jeannine came into the room a couple of minutes later saying she was sorry. Nothing else was said the rest of the night as we fell asleep. The next morning I left early. Jeannine was still sleeping so I didn't say goodbye as I quietly walked out of her room.

As I arrived home I noticed a note folded in half and taped to my door. I curiously removed the note discovering it had been typed from James. His note went into detail about how he no longer valued himself as a person. His sense of self-worth seemed destroyed as he discussed wanting to end his life. The night prior must have really caused him pain. I didn't want to confront him face-to-face just then so I called him instead. As he answered I could tell he was upset. I reassured him I was not going to give up on him and his potential for being a more desirable person to others. James needed me for his growth and because of his unquestionable acceptance of me I needed him.

A few days later I had gotten a call from Jeannine letting me know she was back together with her ex. I was upset due to the abrupt nature of my entire experience with her. I felt as if she played with every emotion I could have had before shutting it down at her discretion. Jeannine was now out of the picture but to my surprise I had apparently made an impression on her roommate. I was given a call from Braxton all of a sudden. She had gotten my number from Jeannine and confessed that she had begun to have feelings for me after meeting me and witnessing how lovingly I treated Jeannine in front of her. Due to my emotional state at the time I decided to find comfort in using Braxton as a substitute for Jeannine.

Round two was about to take place with these girls. Since they lived together I was going to have to get used to seeing Jeannine differently now as a friend. In the beginning it was difficult but my focus on Braxton helped me get over it. She was a hair dresser with multiple tattoos, which I did not care for, but her personality made up for it. We would enjoy relaxed evenings in her home watching movies and playing board games. The duplex the girls lived in was small and full of pets. Braxton had two cats and Jeannine had a dog. The cats were not allowed outside and the dog only went outside to relieve herself.

At first, my OCD was calm in this environment until the dog had accidents in the house. Jeannine had an older dog which seemed to have frequent bowel movements. She would be gone with her ex for extended periods of time, leaving the dog unattended for us to care for. There were times when no one was home and the dog would make messes all over the living room. The messes were primarily on the large area rug, which I avoided like the plague. After realizing the possibility of fecal traces being spread throughout the house, I had to act fast. I decided I would wear two thick socks on each foot every time I entered the home and remove the outer layer when I left. The cat hair also became an issue after witnessing the cat's rolling around on the floor. I knew the hair would eventually get on me due to a cat's tendency to lay on everything.

I coped by constantly using lint brushes to get the hair off my clothes which had to be washed if ever worn again. Needless to say, it got to be too much. After complaining repeatedly to Braxton about the issues in the house I finally let my secret out and told her I had OCD. She was more upset I hadn't told her earlier.

She then in anger put her bare hands in the cat litter box and said, "What are you gonna do now?" In disgust I said I wouldn't be able to ever hold her hand again. She began to cry at the thought of that happening. I told her that this could be fixed but it wouldn't be easy for me to let her know how. She seemed to be open to whatever it was, so I introduced her to my numbered wash chart.

This was the first time ever that I attempted to have somebody other than myself use it. I was very reluctant to have her participate in my odd washing ritual. I felt embarrassed and ashamed at the thought of her doing this. At the same time, I felt her actions brought this on herself which gave me the willingness to make her do it. We got through it and continued the relationship with new understandings of one another.

Braxton was a highly emotional, caring individual with a big heart which made her impulsive with her decision making. As the next month progressed, she became convinced that I was the man she was going to marry. She wanted to persuade me that this idea was to be the next step for us. During trips to the mall she would want to visit jewelry stores. She would browse engagement rings with hopes of creating this false reality of where we were headed. It all got to be too much too soon. I would have to break away from this and leave her.

In an effort to avoid as much drama as possible, I carefully planned my next move with her. Late one night I drove to her home when I knew she would be asleep. Braxton had given me a key to the door. I quietly entered the home and walked into her bedroom. I placed her key on the nightstand and quietly awoke her. She looked up at me in surprise. I then told her I couldn't continue this any longer and wanted to return her key. Before she could say anything I turned away and walked out, locking the front door behind me. I was hoping she wouldn't come running out of the house after me. Fortunately for me, she did not and I was able to flee. I drove off into the night relieved to have her out of my life now. I would be single once again.

Chapter 14

She's The One

After several relationship trail and errors I began to believe I may be incapable of having a long lasting partnership with anyone. My OCD didn't have a lot of time to include someone else. I continued to use MYSPACE to hunt for single women that looked appealing to me. One night before bed while staying with my parents for the weekend I came across a profile of a beautiful young woman named Melissa. She seemed good natured, fun, and enjoyed a lot of the same leisurely activities I did which included my love for watching movies. She was an elementary school teacher, which indicated to me that she was probably patient and caring; a good combination for a guy like me. I would start by sending her a message and friend request. She responded to the next day by playfully asking why she should add me as a friend. I simply replied, "Why not?" and the back and forth correspondence began. We discussed everything from our pursuits in life to our favorite foods. We seemed to hit it off. I would look forward to reading our daily messages from each other after I came home from work. At around one month, I asked if we could exchange phone numbers and she thought it would be a good idea at this point. It was great hearing her voice for the first time. Talking over the phone came so naturally to us because we had become comfortable with one another.

A couple weeks went by and it was time to now meet up in person. I set up a time and place at a nearby restaurant with plans to see a movie afterwards. I was very excited to finally take this step with her. As I arrived and walked up to the restaurant doors...there she was! Melissa was sitting on the bench. Our eyes locked instantly while smiling at one another. "This was it!" I thought to myself as we entered into the building. We went into the less crowded bar area and got a table. I ordered drinks as we began to talking face-to-face. There was such excitement between us. The time seemed to fly by and we had to rush to the movie playing across the street.

We watched a comedy, which got us laughing together. After we left the theater it had become dark. We walked over to our vehicles not knowing what we should do next. I figured we would call it a night, yet we both didn't want it to end. Melissa then invited me over to her apartment where we had deep conservations until the late hours of the night. We discussed religion, relationships, families, and our outlooks on life. The time spent was very meaningful. I then gave her a passionate hug and went home. That one date was really all it took for us. We went dancing together the following weekend at a local club. Shortly after our second date we started our relationship.

The relationship started like all my other ones. I had my space to do my OCD and spent time with Melissa in between. There would be times where my OCD would be more demanding than usual. I would have to cancel our plans to spend time together during these periods. Sometimes there would be little notice given if an OCD issue came up. During this time, I had to make up obligations I had. It was hard doing this because our only time together was on the weekends due to our work schedules. These periods caused friction between us. I wanted to spend time with her but if the OCD didn't come first my mind would be elsewhere obsessing about whatever task that needed to be accomplished. Melissa was very observant and noticed much more than I would have liked. During times where I did push my OCD aside, she would catch me acting distant and ask it something was wrong. I of course denied anything was wrong. This was my way of shielding her from the painful truth I was ashamed to admit. I have tried, on many occasions, to put OCD in the back of my mind while with her and focus on us. Doing this never gave us the kind of quality time what we could have had without it. It was my silent battle, which at times, felt like a screaming voice demanding I take care of it.

I was not about to break the news of my OCD just yet. At around two months it took her observance to finally address it to me. My avoidance to discuss my OCD with her was about to end. It started with a text sent one night while she was out of state visiting an aunt in Las Vegas. The text questioned why I would walk around my car when I arrived at her apartment to see her. The true answer to that question was that the space behind where I would park was contaminated. I was not about to step in that area and spread traces into her apartment. Knowing what was at stake here forced me to walk around rather straight behind my car, which was a much shorter route to her front door.

This text sent caught me off guard. I had thought up until that point that my OCD was pretty well hidden from her. I assumed things between her and I would now take an awkward turn for the worst. It's not easy letting someone you have feelings for know you're mentally ill. Once this type of truth was known there would be no going back. I felt a permanent label would now be placed on me. This realization was too much to bear in the moment. I was ready to text her back and call it quits. I figured I would just move on to another girl until she noticed something then start the process over again.

I was overwhelmed with emotion contemplating how to respond back. I eventually replied back by letting her know I wasn't about to be labeled and thought we should both move on. This approach was random and to the point which shocked her. Melissa then responded by confessing she had started to fall in love with me and saw a future ahead. It then hit me that she was invested in us. Her heartfelt and sincere attempt to keep us together despite my harsh words changed everything.

When she returned home we spoke. To my surprise, she even brought me back a box of my favorite donuts I couldn't get locally. She must really want to keep me around I thought. I opened up about my OCD and explained what I could to her without being overwhelming. To my astonishment Melissa showed a level of compassion I had not received from anyone before. Her patience, sympathy, understanding, and concern for my well-being proved to me her feelings were genuine. I realized that any bumps in the road ahead would only make us stronger. As the months progressed, Melissa really began to understand me and my struggles. Now that she knew what consumed me and my time, there had been less confusion between us. We developed a mutual respect and our bond grew. She accepted me for who I was and showed unconditional love. We connected on a physical, emotional, and intellectual level.

All the pieces I needed were there. Melissa had come to know me better than anyone else in my life. This was possible due to her insistence that I open up about what bothered me. I showed plenty of reluctance in the beginning but she had a way of breaking my silence. It was scary to give her insight into what makes me do what I do. What may be viewed to some as crazy is not easy to talk about. I eventually gave her an all access pass to my mind. The information shared was obviously disturbing but Melissa now knew me completely. She wanted to help anyway she could and was able to help make my life easier by modifying my counting chart.

I had always written my number charts by hand. These charts were pocket size. I kept some in my wallet, others were left at home. They would eventually get wet during washings and need to be replaced. I would then have to spend the time to carefully write out another chart. Melissa was able to create a digital one that could be saved as a computer file and then printed as needed. During the creation of the digital format she also convinced me to minimize the numbers counted on the chart. This would then provide faster wash times when I scrubbed. Even though these alterations didn't provide a complete solution to my OCD, they proved very helpful in relieving my aggravations.

Melissa overlooked my flaws by pointing out everything she loved about me. My willingness to find solutions helped put her at ease when it came to my dysfunctional side. She knew I had potential and her confidence in me help me grow. I finally found someone that had influence over my OCD. The love I felt would inspire me to become a better man for her. She represented all that was worth fighting for. No women had ever had that kind power over me. Melissa had officially become my one and only.

Melissa & I in 2009

Chapter 15

Making It Through When There's Two

They say relationships are work if they are to be long lasting and when you have OCD they are that much harder. Melissa and I have an understanding that she will do what she can to keep my sanity, but she also has to keep her's in the process. I'm aware that I can only ask so much of her when it comes to accommodating me with my OCD. By accommodating me, she goes against what is in her nature to do. She has to act abnormal by request which was not an easy adjustment for her. On the flip side, I must also go against what is in my nature to do for her. Having OCD and acting more normal by request had proven to be just as challenging.

The third world mentioned earlier is what makes us successfully work. Melissa's willingness to live in this world with me is the key to our success together. It's a compromise for the overall good of our relationship with the understanding that I will work toward recovery. My OCD fighting contributions provide some behavioral therapy. The relationship puts myself into situations I am uncomfortable with which includes certain family activities, household chores, and some intimacy. These situations get me to cross the boundaries I put up in an attempt to accept them more. I don't always cooperate and willingly want to partake but make an effort usually. Melissa gives me the strength I need.

My expectations of Melissa are as minimal as I can make them. They include areas and places to avoid, occasional but rare hand washes, and sometimes help in assisting me with a ritual only I do. This does put limitations on her life but she does it out of love for me. There have been OCD escalated moments where she has had to endure more because of a rare incident. This has included times were I have had to OCD wash a belonging of hers or part of her body that had become contaminated. They were the result of circumstances that are out of her control. This occurs when something accidently happens by mistake or someone else does something she must participate in that isn't OCD friendly. I realize she can't be protected all the time from my fears. She has to live her life and I have to be okay with unexpected things happening.

My OCD can't control the world so I must learn to adapt to its unpredictability. Having a game plan for when certain instances occur is a must for us. Melissa and I have the mutual understanding of what OCD task will need to take place if an unexpected event occurs while we are together. These occurrences are usually at stores and restaurants when a clerk or waitress for example drops something to the floor in front of us. Whatever was dropped would have to be something being given to us like money or purchased items. I then make sure I handle the problem by doing the touching from there. I then do the hand washing required instead of her. If contaminated money is ever given to us we deposit it into an ATM we have specifically allocated for this type of issue. Most of the time things go smoothly, but it is necessary for us to have a plan for when they don't.

The common goal is to eventually live a more normal life together. Each step will have to come from me when I am ready but Melissa is willing to put in the time it takes for us to reach that point. There have been plenty of times where I have gotten frustrated enough with myself that I've encouraged Melissa to leave me. I knew in my heart that there could only be two types of love I could ultimately give her. I could love her enough to change some of my ways or love her enough to free her from me and the OCD. We could go our separate ways and she wouldn't have to be burdened by my issues anymore.

I contemplated back and forth for the first couple of years as to what would be in our best interest. I chose our love because I knew it would win in the end. If it meant my OCD had to suffer for our love then I was ready to make that happen for her and us. Her loyalty and support would push me in the right direction. It takes real love to make these kinds of sacrifices for your partner and I am very thankful to have found such a dedicated companion.

Melissa and I have been through a lot together and my OCD can take most of the credit when it comes to the stress in our life. We have endured many OCD influenced obligations I've needed her assistance with. They are always unpleasant but necessary for me. Even though Melissa doesn't partake in most of the actual behaviors, her support helps a great deal with these daunting tasks. She, a lot of times, will be my hands if I need something touched that I cannot do myself in the moment. She also makes special trips with me to uncontaminated locations if I need to purchase something in particular that I must be OCD clean for. When it comes to personal information gathered from our mail or contaminated trash that needs to be taken away, we transport it together.

Living in the city makes it hard to burn big quantities of mail. I generally wait for my local bank to advertise their yearly shredding event which is free to the public. However if I miss it, we then travel to a rural area outside of town and burn it all at an unoccupied campsite with a fire pit. I try to keep what I'm doing from any onlookers since I don't actually pay to use the site. I generally have to find a more isolated area within the campground for such activities. When it comes to contaminated trash I have to handle the removal process with gloves while Melissa drives me to a dumpster to unload it. She has proven to me that we can work as a team when we have to. Melissa has made parts of my life easier this way.

Outside of doing annoying tasks that I've orchestrated, Melissa and I wanted more time together. It was hard due to the fact that I couldn't have her at my place for obvious OCD reasons. I would always be at her place which caused frustrations with her sister whom she lived with. Her sister felt a lack of privacy and was annoyed by my almost 5 days of week presence. As a result we began discussing living together. I had been there and done that before so I knew what it would require. This time around I had nothing to hide. I expressed my need to have a secured room and private wash periods if we were to successfully make this work. Melissa was willing to accommodate me with my requests for now and I couldn't have been more thankful. Spending more time with her would be great for our relationship as long as the OCD had its functioning ability.

We soon found an apartment for us on the east side of town. Melissa moved in first with the help of her parents and me. A closed off room was set aside for me for when I arrived several weeks later. Moving has always been something I've dreaded to do. It requires a tedious preparation period which includes acquiring specific protective tubs from a non-contaminated location. The tubs are used to transport my prized processions, which generally have to be handled with tongs if I choose not to do a thorough OCD hand wash. I have always resisted any help ever offered to me during a move. Risking having someone else contaminate, drop, or place an item or tub somewhere I didn't want would cause extreme anxiety. The frustrations involved would be horrible to put someone else through, so I do it alone for peace of mind.

After an exhausting move, Melissa and I were finally living together. We would now get to see each other every day. It wasn't long before my OCD began to slowly make its presence more noticeable. The neighbor next to us would unintentionally cause this newest issue. Witnessing her constant presence outside her apartment while she allowed her dog to defecate on the walkaway we used was intolerable. This particular neighbor had little respect for herself or others. The unkempt woman regularly wore a bathrobe, sweat pants, and slippers while smoking in front of her door.

I had to stop any contamination from spreading where we walked. I would now have to frequently OCD clean every area I saw droppings from her dog. This process would require removal of the droppings, mitten guards for my hands, antibacterial wipes for scrubbing, and my counting chart. I couldn't have any noise during this procedure so I had to wear earmuffs as well. I was quite a sight to be seen when I had to perform this task outside. It was very uncomfortable for me to be out in the open where anyone could see what I was doing. I frantically did what I had to do. Inevitability curious onlookers observed as they walked by. I just tried to block out everything around me and finish quickly.

My OCD had a way of causing more problems ahead. The sinks in the apartment had faucets that did not extended far enough out for me while washing. This lack of adequate space caused my hands to bump the sides of the sink as I scrubbed and counted. The sink itself could never be viewed as clean since it had contaminated water around it which had splashed off of my unfinished hands. I now had to cautiously OCD wash which made an already agonizing task even worse.

Something had to be done to make my vital washings easier. I eventually resorted to using the wider kitchen sink for my washings. Sharing this sink when Melissa needed it for its intended use was a constant annoyance for both of us. Dishes couldn't be stacked inside the sink, only rinsed and put in the dishwasher carefully. I stressed to her over and over again the importance of never touching or bumping the faucet nozzle while running the water. Eventually she did it by accident, and then I did. Multiple replacement nozzles had to then be purchased at my expense.

Washing in the kitchen sink got even worse as I carelessly allowed my wet unfinished hands to drip water onto the counter space around the sink. This occurred when I would reach for the soap pump using my wrists in between sections I was washing. It is hard being patient during an OCD wash. I wanted to get it done as soon as possible. Making sure to shake excess water off my hands every time I needed to reach out for more soap was not always on my mind to do. My impatience led to contaminated water getting all over the kitchen counter area where I had washed. Now part of our kitchen was contaminated and unable to be used. Nothing could be placed there. I kept telling Melissa I would fix it, but the area was too large to properly OCD clean and make usable again. In an effort to temporarily fix the problem I placed several plastic garbage bags on top of the contaminated areas so we could have the counter space back. The kitchen now looked messy and I felt embarrassed looking at it. It was a constant reminder to Melissa my OCD was out of control.

Due to my OCD issues surrounding our home. It was time for a change. We had to find a pet free living situation and a home with extended length faucets in the bathrooms. It had to be OCD friendly to work for us.

We knew what to look for and found a duplex in a quite area of town. It had everything we needed. The madness that plagued me would get some relief. We just had to move again, which was never easy, but would make our life significantly better once it was done. This time around, I wanted no outside help from anyone other than Melissa and me. Ideally it would have been helpful to have family lend a hand with our heavier items we both used. This of course could not happen due to my OCD. Other than Melissa, they would never understand my irrational ways and wouldn't want to be a part of the insanity. My OCD couldn't allow anything of ours to be destroyed in my mind, even though physically nothing would happen.

It was all up to us. I would have to do my usual prep work. I also planned on renting a moving van to first transport my more protected items while the vehicle was considered clean. Then use the van to move the rest of what we had. A couple of days prior to our move, I came across a moving van at our apartment complex from the same company I planned on using. There was no way I was going to risk renting that same van that was now being used here. I knew whoever was renting the van would walk on the contaminated ground and into the van while moving. I quickly wrote down the license plate number so I would know the van not to rent.

The day of the move arrived. There ended up being only one rental company around with two locations in town. I thought it would be best to rent from the location furthest from the apartment to reduce the likelihood of that one particular van being there. We purposely drove across town to pick up what I considered would be a clean rental van. To my horror I noticed there was only one van available on the lot and it had that same license plate number! It felt like I was being punished. My caution and careful planning was never going to work. Melissa was very frustrated with me. We then drove to the closer location and rented a van there. We were not off to a great start.

I took a great deal of time meticulously loading the van with only my prized processions. Melissa drove the van to our duplex while I watched over everything in the back. Once at the duplex I again had to carefully unload all my stuff. Melissa helped open doors as I stressfully began hauling the belongings from the van to my new secured room. This was a job only I could do. Melissa's small contributions to my cause were very much appreciated during this time. She knew the level of mental strain I was under was intense. If anything were to go wrong during this transport process, my OCD would strike with vengeance. Thanks to Melissa's patience and my diligence I completed the process without incident. The hardest part of our move was over. The sense of relief was so overwhelming, similar to escaping death. It all may sound ridiculous, but this is what my OCD does to me.

Over the next 12 hours we moved the rest of our stuff. The do or die feelings were gone at this point, but we still had to be careful not to drop or place anything were it shouldn't be. We hauled loads late into the evening which then progressed into the morning. We were about ready to pass out from exhaustion when we finally were finished.

All the hard work and craziness on my part paid off. Our new place worked out just the way we hoped it would. The layout of the duplex suited us well. Melissa could now have an aesthetically pleasing home. I had my one secured room and the bathroom washing areas were OCD approved. Our one neighbor next to us was quiet and had no pets. Everything worked out for the best and my OCD was a lot more tolerable in the home.

Chapter 16

The Family Effect Part 2

While there are parts of my OCD that have gotten better over time, other parts have expanded and gotten worse. My contamination fears slowly spread to Melissa's family in much the time way they did with my own. I blame myself for initially causing the problem. Instead of monitoring the types of shoes we were wearing to insure they had not been used on a contaminated floor, I got careless. Contamination was now going to be introduced into Melissa's family. It started with the floors of her parent's home. Like always, things are eventually dropped, items are placed on the floor, and people are on the floor which spread the traces from that area and got everywhere. Unfortunately, it does not matter how clean something can appear. Once it is contaminated in my mind there is no going back without major dysfunctional behaviors being involved to fix it. I can't ask normal people to have OCD to make me calmer, so I just enter my dirty world with them.

The problem is I don't want to be in that world longer than I have to. I can, of course, deal with it and most of the time I am able to not make a scene in front of people when I am aggravated. Melissa's family is more observant than mine so it is hard to not look distraught when I am having an issue around them. On many occasions I have been asked by Melissa's parents if I was okay, or why I was being so quiet. They knew nothing of my OCD at the time.

Melissa and I thought it would be best to keep my OCD a secret from her family for as long as possible. No parent wants to hear that their daughter is in a relationship with a mentally ill man. My kind of illness had to be slowly introduced as things happened.

Things would definitely happen as time passed. It got to be too apparent that something was going on and explanations were imminent. A camping trip including her parents, two sisters, and brother would finally reveal my disorder years after our relationship had begun.

Summer had arrived and it was time to spend it with Melissa's side of the family. Melissa's parents had a large travel trailer and invited us to camp near them. We traveled south down the I-5 interstate to Ashland, then headed northeast into the mountains until we reached our destination at Howard Prairie Lake. When we arrived, it began to rain so we waited for the weather to clear before putting up our tent. We didn't want to sit in the car or be out in the rain. This meant we would have to seek shelter in the trailer with her entire family inside. I immediately began to panic knowing I would not be allowed to wear my wet shoes in the trailer. My shoes were my protection from the floors of my now dirty world I was about to enter again. Melissa hoped her mom would just let me wipe my shoes on their rug before entering. I assured Melissa this wouldn't happen, but she wanted to try anyway. We got out of the car as it rained on us. We hastily walked over to the trailer and knocked on the door. Her mother opened the door and greeted us. Just as I predicted she then asked us to take off our shoes. I knew this was coming and said I'd be back, not knowing what I was going to do next. I knew I would not be returning to the trailer if something wasn't done to accommodate my OCD.

I then ran out into the rain and got back into the car. I just sat there for several minutes trying to come up with a solution. As time passed I also worried about how this looked to everyone. I eventually came up with a plan to wear several layers of socks on my feet. After looking through my bag I didn't have enough socks of my own to give me adequate protection. I then had to walk back to the trailer and ask for Melissa to come out. I knew this behavior looked strange but I felt I had no choice. Melissa came out of the trailer crying due to this entire ordeal. I felt ashamed and sad for her. I asked if she had some extra socks I could use. She had some heavy wool socks that ended up working for me. Melissa's tears had to be explained somehow so she told everyone I had OCD while I was prepping myself in the car. Fifteen minutes later my aggravations were put to rest and I was able to join everyone in the trailer. Nothing was mentioned about what had just been revealed. All I could do was try to lighten the mood through positive conversation.

The sun came out and we were then able to find a presumably clean area to place our tent. This area was necessary because the tent had to be placed on the ground in order for us to put it together. I couldn't have any help from anyone other than Melissa; otherwise the tent would be contaminated, making it hard for me to feel comfortable while sleeping in it. Fortunately for my OCD no one offered.

During our camping trip, I would on many occasions leave abruptly and wash my hands in a nearby restroom. This was necessary from time to time when I was in my dirty world with the rest of the family. These washes had to be done when I needed to put on clean clothes or use an item that was not being thrown away after the trip. I limited my restroom visits as much as I could, but the length of my time gone was often noticed. There had even been a time where I was walked in on while washing by Melissa's dad. I wasn't about to keep washing and counting like a weirdo in front of him. I just had to leave and come back shortly. They were necessary annoyances that had to be done to conceal what I was actually doing.

One particularly uncomfortable moment occurred when a family member dropped a letter to the ground. Now if the letter had landed in an area we hadn't walked on, then no contamination would have occurred. Unfortunately the letter dropped directly onto a path where we all had stepped. I was the only one who had noticed the dropped letter. The thought of someone picking up that letter was too much for me to handle. I knew I was in my dirty world so I quickly picked it up and tossed it in the fire pit. I didn't want to wait for someone else to pick it up; otherwise it would just reconfirm my contamination fears towards the family. I knew I could wash what I had just done away and be fine. Of course later on there was question as to where the letter had gone. I just had to play stupid.

The camping trip was about to come to a close. Melissa and I began taking down the tent. This time Melissa's dad offered to help us. I didn't have it in me to tell him to stop. He did not know the extent of my OCD at that time and was just trying to be helpful. This caused an immediate panic and I had to stop helping them both. I froze in fear knowing the tent would now never be able to be used again. I had no way to OCD wash an entire tent! I just stood there watching them both roll up the tent. The rest of the family stared at me wondering what the hell I was doing in that moment. I felt as if the tent had just caught fire and was watching it burn. This could have all been avoided if I had just spoken up. But speaking up would have made things awkward as well. In the future I would need to choose the lesser of the two evils when it came to matters like this.

Overall the camping trip was stressful. I had now made my odd behaviors officially known to my other family with a label to go along with it. I knew it was just of matter of time before my true self would make its presence known. It's hard to be seen as less desirable to someone when you had a different image in the beginning, especially when it involves family.

Our families would always have their opinions. For the most part, I felt support with concerns here and there. I felt Melissa's family put had put their faith in her decision to be with me. My family on the other hand knew a great deal more about my OCD. They were all concerned for Melissa. The concerns would make themselves known during visits to my parent's place. It began with my sister who privately briefed Melissa on what she was getting herself into. I had come clean about my OCD at that point so the information shared was no shock to her. My parent's would also have private discussions with her while I was momentarily away.

The OCD aspect of things had to be addressed. After moving away from my parents I decided it would be best to keep my OCD private by not bringing it up. I didn't want them to worry anymore. I would only visit them a few times a year at best, so that was the last thing I wanted to discuss. I preferred keeping my dysfunctional side to myself. As a result of my silence on the subject, they felt a need to have Melissa fill them in on how I was doing. I eventually grew tired of these types of inquiries given behind my back. I understood their need to know...but they could have asked me, also. I suppose they probably thought Melissa would give them a more fair assessment than I. Being honest I'd have to say they were right. I would generally make things out to be better than they were. During one of these private chats, I purposely intervened. I wanted to let my family know that I was aware. After my feelings were heard I made an effort to be more open with them.

Chapter 17

What Has Come To Be

Life, thus far, has been a nonstop ride consisting of me, the OCD, and the people around me whom have either played a permanent or temporary role in it. These people, who have come into my life for one reason or another, have given me unforgettable experiences. It was hard to let go of Camille after our engagement failed. While single I attempted to contact her years later. We met up a few times and couldn't seem to start again where we had left off. All eventually was put to rest between us. It occurred in a profound way as the result of a random encounter. I had been dating Melissa and her and I both crossed paths with Camille on our way out of a movie theater. I hadn't seen her in years. She was with her parents and they all had just finished watching the same movie as us. I gave her an uncomfortable hug and introduced her to Melissa. They shook hands which to me symbolized a type of finalization to my past with her. This introduction affected me in a profound way. My old love could now be introduced to what would be my new love. It was a bittersweet ending after what she had put me through.

James graduated from the University of Oregon with a Bachelor's degree in music performance. After I left the studio apartment complex we shared, it had become harder to stay in touch with one another. A lot of my time was now being spent with Melissa. James followed in my footsteps and met a girl online and is now in a serious relationship. He and I check in on one another from time to time. He will always be a dear friend to me.

Melissa and I are happily engaged with plans to be married in a year. I proposed to her on a trip we took to Alaska. We flew there during her spring break from work. I kept a ring she had picked out in my pocket waiting for the opportune moment. Our visit to Denali National Park provided the perfect setting. The skies were clear and a vast landscape of mountains surrounded us with their majestic beauty. I knelt down carefully in the snow, pulled out the ring, and recited a few lines describing what she meant to me.

Melissa teared up, grinning with emotion and said yes! We have a summer wedding planned.

I see many obstacles yet ahead. Raising a family of my own will have its own challenges. Babies will crawl on the floor and diapers will have to be changed. I will have to cope somehow someway with my OCD. Luckily I will have nine months of pregnancy to prepare myself for when that happens. I have hope that as the years go by I will have discovered and practiced enough solutions for my OCD that my suffering decreases and I am able to embrace life more. I have been blessed to have found Melissa. I know now that a life shared where there are joint emotions, experiences, and challenges create a much more meaningful existence for me. I feel she will give me the strength and patience to rise above for the greater good.

I've come to firmly believe that my life is happening for me and not to me. It is up to me to discover its complete meaning. No one else has to live in your mind but you. Its complexity has to be broken down, understood, and made more functional for me. I feel I was given OCD for a reason and I must rise above from what has held me down for so long. I don't want to dwell on all the fixes I anticipate will need to happen as a whole. I will need to block out any overwhelming deterrents and focus on what's next. A simplistic approach that would create a step-by-step process for going forward is the ultimate goal. It can start by placing day-to-day emphasis on specific areas. These areas will need to include some type of therapy, medication, and coping strategy. Relaxing the mind through meditation has also interested me. Through my experience these are key and my best recommendation for those recovering from various types of OCD. This recovery process for me involves a rewiring of my brain. I have analyzed, altered, and practiced my OCD for decades. My mind has become accustom to functioning in the way I've taught it to for all those years. I unfortunately cannot just erase or reprogram everything I've developed in mind as a result of my OCD. I do currently take medication and it does help control the intensity of my thoughts and reduces my stress. What has to be determined is type of prescription drug needed and the proper dosage amount to take. Once I am married and sharing health insurance it hopefully will be more affordable for me to again seek another psychiatrist for further assistance. Until then, I will continue to carry on the best way I can.

At the very moment I started writing this book I felt an unbelievable ability to express myself to you the reader. I fully believe it was my calling to share my story with you. Writing this book has been a therapeutic journey into my past, present, and possible future of my life with OCD. I have kept many parts of my mental illness hidden until writing this book. I had to reach an acceptance level to really open myself up to the harsh reality that is my life with OCD. Examining my current state as well as what led up to it has given me clarity to see the big picture. I plan to discover my true potential in time more clearly. Being truly alive and well can no longer seem like a luxury for me, it must be a reality. Deep down in my soul I believe our bodies are shells used to experience the world around us. I have been fixated on maintaining my body's shell and material things, which in turn keeps me from having the complete human experience. Our time on Earth is limited and precious. My OCD has taken so much from me and I know I can't get the time back I've wasted. Going forward I hope my OCD can now give back through this book by reaching out to others who are suffering. I know I am not alone, even though it has felt that way in my mind. According to The National Institute of Mental Health, OCD affects about 2.2 million American adults. Many of those adults do not get proper help and resort to homelessness. The American health care system must also provide affordable options which are lacking today.

I'm not a success story but I understand OCD and the road one must take to recover. I feel this is where you have to start to be on the right path.. I have my own unique version of this mental illness and have been personalizing my recovery plan based on what has been proven to work. I will not give up on myself because I know there is a big beautiful world out there for me to enjoy. I know the steps in front of me will be hard at times but my determination to succeed has always driven me forward into the light. My life can no longer be defined by my OCD. There is hope, if you just put everything about yourself into perspective, focus, and in your heart know what matters most!

Life is what you make of it...full of positive and negative parts. It is what you decide to do with both that will ultimately determine your level of happiness! -Derek

www.ingramcontent.com/pod-product-compliance
Lightning Source LLC
Chambersburg PA
CBHW070535290526
45790CB00002B/502